MW01026496

An Addict in the Family

A Mother's Tale of Heartbreak, Courage and Resilience

Stephanie Hammond

Delahoyde Publishing Co Ltd

Copyright © 2023 by Stephanie Hammond

All rights reserved.

No part of this book may be reproduced, stored in a retrieval system, or transmitted in any form or by any electronic or mechanical means including photocopying, recording, or otherwise, without prior permission in writing from the author, except for fair use..

ISBN 978-0-473-68203-3 Paperback

ISBN 978-0-473-68204-0 Kindle

ISBN 978-0-473-68205-7 PDF

Contents

DEDICATION

To my grandson, Darrius, who called from Germany, heard my distress and sent his cousin to my rescue.

To CareNZ Community Services, Hamilton, New Zealand who has the understanding and vision to establish the Whanau Group, a group whose purpose is to support those who are trying to support loved ones in the throes of addiction.

To all members of the Whanau Group, past, current and future and to your loved one who is caught in the web of addiction.

And to my husband whose strength, insight and never wavering love sustains me through the joys and trials of life.

... grant me the ... courage to change the things I can...

ACKNOWLEDGEMENTS

Members of the CareNZ Whānau Group

Sherryn Hill, Facilitator of the CareNZ Whānau Group

Mabruka, Manager, CareNZ Community Services, Hamilton

Finally, I acknowledge:
All those who supported me as I struggled to support Charlie; and
All who read and commented on the numerous drafts. Your help is invaluable.

AUTHOR'S NOTE

N ames and some identifying details have been changed to protect the privacy of people mentioned and involved.

GLOSSARY

Thruppence 3 pennies in pre-decimal currency in Australia and the United Kingdom

Farthing a quarter of a penny in pre-decimal currency in Australia and the United Kingdom

Pounamu is a precious and powerful New Zealand greenstone, often carved into a pendant or necklace, which carries special meaning for its wearer.

Skip Bin is a waste bin brought to, and taken away from, the site by a waste disposal company. Contaminated material is treated off-site before being disposed of in an appropriate facility.

The following are taken from Te Aka at WWW.maor idictionary.co.nz/dictionary-info

Tangi Shortened form of *tangihanga*. Rites for the dead - a Māori funeral ceremony – literally to cry, mourn, weep over.

Whānau extended family, family group, a familiar term of address to a number of people – the primary economic unit of traditional Māori society. In the modern context the term is sometimes used to include friends who may not have any kinship ties to other members.

INTRODUCTION

I could have chosen any experience in my full and adventurous life to write about. So why choose to write about my efforts to support my son while he was in the throes of the consequences of his addiction to methamphetamine?

Perhaps deep down the answer lies in the hope that one day he will read this – my statement on the way his addiction has impacted me and our family – and will know the depth of my love for and acceptance of him, regardless of the journey he is on.

During this time, I met countless others who were as desperate to save their loved ones from the effects of their addictions. Like me, they found themselves lost in a system ill-equipped to provide the type of help and support we needed.

My hope is that others caught in the web of a loved one's addictions will read my story and gain hope, along with some insight, into how their lives can still be purposeful and joyous even though they can't see through the grief of the moment. I firmly believe there is a path to connection and support for them too.

In the process of writing, I have examined afresh the depths of addiction my own family has been caught in through the generations. Although not so obvious, or as socially unacceptable, my own addictions, like I suspect are Charlie's, are steeped in the effects of early emotional trauma. I hint at those effects of my own early experiences in the first chapter.

In my search to help Charlie I have found a way to heal myself. It's early days yet, but I have found a way to face the emotions of my own trauma and am finding the strength to abstain from my own addictive substances, one day at a time, and with support.

In the end, I hope that what I've written will be a conversation starter leading to awareness of the widespread effects of addiction and paving the way for change. Change in the way society views addiction; change in the way those addicted view their place in the hearts of those who are most affected by their actions; and change in the availability and type of support systems that all those touched by addiction so desperately need.

CHAPTER ONE

Toowoomba, Australia
1950s

I *am three-years- old*

I'm here in the kitchen, alone, again. I press my hands over my ears as my mother's shrill laughter echoes through the wall. I should be in bed. I can't sleep like my older brother can. I try to let the music fill my body, drowning the voices sounding in my ears.

I lie on the floor in front of the big wooden stove bathed in its warmth. I rock to the music. The adults are singing along, with happy harmonies. "Forever and ever," they croon and I'm remembering picking wild mushrooms with my daddy along the side of the racing track behind our house. Early in the morning the horses aren't racing and we're safe. On race day my cousin Daphne and I climb through the fence and lie as close as we dare to the edge of the track. My heart jumps into my throat as I feel the thunder of horses' hooves. I look at Daphne's face to decide if I stay or follow my urge to run away. She's excited, breathing hard and as soon as the horses burst into view, their massive muscles straining, she jumps up and shouts at the jockeys, "Stop whipping them, you bullies!" Then the horses are gone, and we lie back on the grass, laughing. We're safe.

I remember Daddy cooking the mushrooms we've picked in the fry pan. He cuts thick slices of bread and sticks the toasting fork in and lets me toast the bread over the flames. I never tell him I hate mushrooms. I eat anything he offers, just to be with my daddy.

The singing gets louder. My ears hurt. I climb onto the table and crawl over to the sugar bowl. I'll get into trouble again, I know. My mother only gives us sweets on special occasions. It's not allowed, me eating the sugar. She never asks me why. Would I have the words to explain? If I tried, would she understand how I don't hear the voices and I'm not afraid when I eat the sugar?

I'll just play with the sugar I tell myself. At first, it's enough. The sugar runs through my fingers and muffles the voices. I imagine playing in the street with the cousins. Tomorrow is Sunday School day and I'll be up before everyone, first dressed and ready to go. Sunday School is the safest place. I love going with the older cousins. I'm learning to be kind and to be good. I love the stories of Jesus and the little children. When I grow up, I'll be a good person, like I'm learning at Sunday School. Mum doesn't come. She doesn't see us stop at the corner store and spend a little bit of the thruppence we are each given for the offering plate. No one checks how much we put in the plate. I buy a milky coconut ice block and a gobstopper, a farthing each.

The music gets louder. There's a crash and I jump. The laughing is louder too now. There's clinking of glasses. My tummy hurts and I feel wheezy. In the mornings, my daddy wheezes. Then he coughs and coughs until I think he'll turn inside out. I scrape some butter with my finger and dip it into the sugar bowl and then into my mouth. My mouth closes around the end of my finger and I breathe easier. *This feels so good*.

I don't know how long I'm here, on the table, dipping my finger into the butter, into the sugar, into my mouth. Again, and again. The pain goes and I stop hearing the voices. The sugar bowl is empty. I fall asleep, there on the table, cocooned in the warm comfort of a settled tummy.

I don't feel Daddy pick me up. I don't smell his beery breath. I don't feel him stumble as he carries me to my room. I don't feel him tuck me into bed. I don't hear the noises. I don't hear my parents' angry voices. I don't hear their fighting. I'm safe. I'm safe now.

·····••·····

I am ten-years-old

After the death of his father, Dad drank more heavily and almost daily. While drunk, he tucked our little sister behind his shoulder as he took her for a drive in the car. Mum became afraid for our little sister's safety and decided to leave. Even though I was only ten years old, Mum gave me the choice to stay with Dad or go with her. I wanted to stay. Not with Dad so much, but there among my cousins, in our street and home that were familiar and at the school I loved. But she made it clear she would take our little sister with her. I know now that my brother and I were too young to make that choice. However, we knew from bitter experience how much we needed each other when the drinking got out of hand. We had a little conference and together we agreed that we would go with Mum and do all in our power to protect our sister and each other.

Events of that first year away from Toowoomba scarred my brother and me for life. By the second year, we were living in the old US Army barracks that had been turned into accommodation for the poor, predominantly single mothers and their children. In the 1950s, our 'housing estate' was an embarrassing blot on a city struggling to overcome a 'brutal housing shortage' – written of years later as *the slum huts that shamed Brisbane*.

CHAPTER TWO
New Zealand, 2019

I drive along the motorway reflecting on my visit with my friend Sue. We'd been friends for years and our meet-ups at the motorway service centre café were always a joy, catching each other up on our writing projects, our family doings, and our own emotional wellbeing. The car phone rings. It's my son's partner, Jessica. "Charlie's been arrested. He's in court tomorrow. Can you come? Please? He needs his Mum."

I grip the steering wheel, hardly registering the rest of the call. Tears streaming, I pull onto the motorway shoulder and turn off the engine. I slump over the steering wheel and try to breathe. I fumble with the car door and my legs crumble as I try to stand. Bent double, crouched low on the ground, my only thought *I have to get home*. I crawl back into my seat, stuff some peppermints into my mouth and open the packet of ginger nut biscuits on the passenger seat. *I need to block my thoughts. Turn up the music. Don't think. Just drive.*

I pull out into the traffic. Scenes of life with Charlie flash through my mind: The impish boy, bringing laughter and joy with him everywhere he goes. Resilience is there too. Concussion from a hockey stick leads to a stay in hospital. He is back on the field the next club day. And sensitive, his gentle eyes locking on mine as he hands me flowers and declares his undying love.

Charlie is the youngest of my middle three children. There's two-and-a-half years between the oldest boy and Charlie, with a girl in between. Without the help of my two older daughters, I'm sure neither Charlie nor I would have survived a pregnancy fraught with illness. Survive he did, and thrived, toddling around after his older siblings, willing to join in their games, playing whatever role they gave him. Years later came two more daughters and Charlie became the protective, loving older sibling.

Where has that Charlie disappeared to? Did it start the day, at 14-years-old, he faced suspension from school? He lived with his father then; he paid school fees only for those of our children who lived with him. Charlie responded to my offer to talk to the principal with, "F**k off out of my life, Mum!" I reached out to him. He flung his fists out, squared shoulders thrust towards me. To this day I regret letting his anger and my fear drive me away. What would be different if I'd taken him in my arms then, as I longed to?

That day seems a lifetime ago and yet those memories are so clear. The decades have taken their toll. On him, on me, on our family. And now Charlie is in prison. Our family tried to stay close to him, to bring him into our circle of love, but he rarely responded. How I wish this poem shared by his sister had been prophetic:

Outwitted
He drew a circle that shut me out
Heretic, rebel, a thing to flout.

But love and I had the wit to win:
We drew a circle and took him in!
- Edwin Markham

Was my love not strong enough? Was I so slow witted I missed the signals that he was not coping? On the rare occasions I visited Charlie at his home, I felt an intruder, ignorant of how the drug scene enveloped his life.

"He'll be an alcoholic," my mother had predicted of the preschool Charlie. An evil thing to say, I accused her. Yet alcohol was a problem for him until he swore off it when he turned 40. And the cannabis he'd taken since his mid-teens went next. He could discard those drugs, but it was the hard drugs that landed him here in prison. Could I have foreseen this? Could I have helped? What sort of mother was I?

How I wished I'd had a healthier relationship with my own mother. I would have asked her what she saw in Charlie to make her say he'd be an addict. I'd ask her what she would advise to make sure her prediction didn't come true. But I never gave her the opportunity to say more, to share her own experience. She certainly had knowledge of addiction I never knew about. And I shut her down.

I reach for another ginger nut. The packet is empty. Soon I am home.

··········

The buzz of the waiting area washes around me. People crowd into the seats by the windows and disappear as case names and courtroom numbers are called on the speakers.

Charlie's case is scheduled for ten o'clock. I speak only when comments or questions come my way. I munch on the ever-present peppermints.

Ten o'clock comes and goes. Finally, the speaker crackles. "Hooper. Courtroom 3. Starts in five minutes." Signs on the door and on the walls inside the courtroom remind us to turn off our mobile phones. It's gone eleven o'clock and the process is starting at last.

I sit in the gallery surrounded by several of Charlie's supporters. His sister, my middle daughter, and his stepsister. There's also Jessica and her mother. Two friends I know from his teenage years. One is his housemate. None of the others I know.

Charlie is in the dock, flanked by burly officers in Corrections uniforms. I see another part of the little boy Charlie now. Scared, unsure of what he's in trouble for this time. I want to talk to him, to comfort him. I try to catch his eye. He seems unaware of us sitting to his left, behind the clear plastic screen. I will him to look my way, but he stares straight ahead. He leans forward, picking at his nails, his left knee jiggling.

Charlie's court appointed lawyer rushes in and takes his seat. Is he overworked? Is his time management poor? Is lateness a tactic he uses for effect? Is his lateness the reason Charlie's session didn't start on time?

Today, I'm annoyed at his tardiness. I had hoped to have a word with him before court. *He has presence though*, I think. He knows we are there in the gallery. As he presents Charlie's case, he waves his arm at us. "Charlie has the support of his family and friends", he tells the judge. How does he know we are all there for Charlie? I wonder how well prepared he is. Is this a variety of a common argument he uses? I know the judge is perceptive. If Charlie accepted wholesome support from this many people, he'd neither use nor deal in drugs.

The matter of bail is raised. The name of Charlie's best friend, Nina, is put forward. The police officer assigned to Charlie's case tells the judge the police do not support bail to her because she is 'suspected of being a user'. My daughter shakes her head, "Not true!" she hisses.

No suitable bail residence being offered, Charlie is remanded to stay in prison. A future hearing date is set. A guard glares at me and points to the sign on the wall as I open my phone to put the date in my calendar. I make a mental note to bring pen and paper next time.

Jessica walks beside me as we file out of the courtroom, down the stairs, out of the building. "Can I put your name up for bail for Charlie?" I agree.

The others are congregating at the foot of the courtroom steps on the side of the road. I sit on the wall and listen. I hear mention of a meeting. "What's this?" I ask.

My middle daughter hesitates. "Nina and Peter invited us to their place to discuss things." I tilt my head and raise my eyebrows. "Do you want to come?" she asks.

"Text me the time and address."

·········

T he house is architecturally designed in a middle-class neighbourhood. Well-kept lawns, electric gates, and an expensive car create an air of affluence. Inside, Nina's home is spotless. *Either Nina is fastidious or has a cleaner,* I think.

Nina is deep in conversation with my daughter when I enter. I meet Nina's husband, Peter. I wait for Jessica to arrive, but learn she isn't invited. We are joined by Charlie's daughter and her husband, his stepsister and housemate.

"You know I never liked Jessica. Isn't that right Peter?" Nina ignores us as we take our seats. She continues explaining her view of Jessica. "This is all her fault." According to Nina, Jessica is selfish, money hungry, caring first for herself and her son and what she can get out of Charlie. "She's too young for him. She says Charlie's house will be hers when he dies. Hers and her son's"

I lean forward and put my hand on hers. "All this talk about Jessica behind her back makes me really uncomfortable, Nina."

She turns away and, instead of quieting her tirade, she brings up more and more "proof" about Jessica's shortcomings. I look at the others for signs they also are uncomfortable at Nina's words. No one meets my eyes.

I tune out. She is immaculately dressed and her makeup flawless. My eyes roam the open plan living area. I note the quality drapes and furniture. The tasteful paintings on the wall. A home nurse I met told me how some addicts keep up appearances to prove how in control of their lives they are. They believe their substance use doesn't affect their ability to function. My mother always looked after her appearance, too. Regardless of how poor we were, even in second hand clothes, she was immaculate.

I suspect there is more truth than not in the police officer's reasons for refusing Charlie to be bailed to Nina's care.

Her voice rises, bringing me back to the table. According to Nina, "More than once, Jessica sat in my garage kitchen with her scales and drugs and bagged the little crystal beads of meth." If this is true, I think it would also be true that Nina was complicit.

"What did Charlie say about it? Why didn't you tell the cops she brought methamphetamine into your home?" She stares at me and shakes her head. A thought niggles at me and for the first time, I wonder why the police arrested only Charlie.

Peter brings out a bag of jewellery. The day before the arrest Jessica asked him to safeguard it. "Stolen. Or exchanged for drugs, most likely," Peter says. There are bracelets and watches, all good quality and new.

I ask Peter what the police said about the items and why they didn't take them.

"I'll take them to them later if things don't go well for Charlie. Insurance. Proof against her if we need it."

I shake my head. This is strange logic indeed. Incidentally, these items never surface again, even when 'things don't go well' for Charlie.

Peter agrees with Nina. Charlie would never involve himself in hard drugs except for Jessica's influence. He sums up Nina's argument. "Jessica masterminded the whole business. In the end, she informed on him. She has history of latching on to a guy for his potential to give her what she wants and then when the source dries up, she gives the police information to lock him up. Charlie's turn this time."

Someone may have informed on Charlie, and it may have been Jessica – or perhaps the police were more astute and were already aware of his dealing and watching his house? The month before they arrested Charlie, the police executed several drug raids resulting in multiple arrests. It is likely Charlie was a casualty of police diligence.

Still, was Jessica the cause of Charlie's dealing? Or was it a natural extension of his addiction? To pay for his drugs? And did his methamphetamine use stem from the death of his baby thirteen years previously? That horrific event is never far from my thoughts.

I'd come home from abroad for a visit, looking forward to meeting six months old Johnny. Charlie's then wife refused to let me see him; Charlie didn't argue.

A few weeks later, I was mountain climbing with my daughter in Australia when Charlie called. "Johnny's dead," tears choked his voice. "I'm sorry I didn't fight to let you meet him, mum." We cried with him. The next day we flew home for the tangi where I had the opportunity to finally meet Johnny. I came to know and love him as I sat there for hours, holding his cold little hands that felt alive in mine. I immersed my thoughts in what might have been, what should have been. A cot death, Sudden Infant Syndrome, SIDs. Here, lying so peaceful in his open casket, Johnny looked robust and healthy. *What happened to you, Johnny?* The unanswerable question.

Charlie admitted his drug use escalated after Johnny's death and he and his wife often self-medicated with cannabis and alcohol. But he never mentioned other drug use.

Johnny's passing also heralded the death of Charlie's marriage. When I returned from overseas a couple of years later, Charlie appeared more withdrawn from the family and, although pleasant enough when I saw him, he never initiated contact. Unknown to me then, methamphetamine had a strong hold and his associates and friends were also users. By this time his marriage was over, and Jessica was his new partner.

I say none of this at Nina and Peter's house. But I wonder why they blame Jessica for his drug use as if taking drugs is a new thing for Charlie.

The day of the arrest the police searched his house, seizing incriminating items: cannabis, a high quantity of methamphetamine, scales and baggies, three mobile phones, and a large quantity of money - all indicative of dealing. They also found weapons: a taser and pepper spray. His housemate and Jessica were searched but the police did not implicate them in the crimes.

We are at Nina and Peter's house to discuss what happened after the police took Charlie into custody. Jessica's family were waiting in the street with cars and trailers. As soon as the police left the property with Charlie, they drove in and took away several loads of his furniture. The housemate called my daughter who arrived in time to stop further pilfering. Nina and Peter also arrived to help. None of those items were ever recovered.

"Your daughter saved the rest of Charlie's furniture, Stephanie," Peter says. "She took charge and ordered Jessica's family off the property." I could see her doing just that, my daughter who has such strength and courage. I smiled at the image. My no-nonsense daughter with a heart of gold and the whānau's interests uppermost. *If he accepts her support, things will turn out well for Charlie*, I think.

CHAPTER THREE

I seek to understand and to be understood

During these long weeks as I start to navigate this new world, I lose sight of the strong capable woman I'm used to seeing in myself. Officers at the prison talk to me as if I'm a child or answer my questions by pointing to a list of resources on the wall. Organisations I'm directed to have no understanding of methamphetamine use. I google and research and finally seek answers from the people I meet, strangers as well as friends. I need the human connection.

To anyone who will listen to me, I say, "My son's been arrested. For methamphetamine use and dealing." I get the sense that my words are the opening so many people are looking for to unburden their own hearts. They tell me of similar experiences; we have a common bond. They're from all walks of life. They're my long-term friends and they are random acquaintances. Everyone, it seems, has stories of coping with a loved one's addiction.

Ellen's story tugs at my heart. Her brother had twice been bailed to her place. He'd asked to be bailed to her, which surprised her. "We'd drifted apart over the years," she said. "But he'd chosen me because he knew I could help him. He knew I wouldn't put up with that nonsense." But she often found drug using paraphernalia, sometimes in the garage, other times in the rubbish bin. Brand new items turned up in her living room. Boxes full of books and clothing. All stolen. She was always on edge. One day she found methamphetamine crystals in a dish in his wardrobe. "I lost it then. I threw everything out the window. The wardrobe, bedding, bed, his clothing, everything. All of it went out the window. I was so angry at him." He chose the drugs over getting his life together and ended in prison the third time. She hardly sees him now and as far as she knows, he's still using.

When I mention we are contemplating bail, no one is encouraging. They share their own horror stories: of their loved one breaking bail; of abuse, theft, unwelcome visitors; and of drug use in their home. They tell of finding guns under mattresses.

Although the stories and messages are varied; the advice is the same. "Don't do it!" "Turn your back and run." "Addicts are all the same." "He'll never change." "He'll rob you blind." And most fearful to me, "He'll destroy your marriage."

When I finally talk with Charlie about bail, he is loving and sorry. He's committed to change. I ignore the warnings and my husband agrees that we can be assessed for our suitability.

We welcome the Corrections Officers into our home. First is the security person. Assessing the house itself for suitability is straightforward. Charlie will wear an electronic monitoring device. The signal can be read from every part of the property and clear boundaries can be monitored from the control area. So technically, bail can be granted to our house.

Next, we are interviewed for our personal suitability. The interviewer is not inspiring. At the end of the interview, she pushes a form across to us. "If," she emphasises the word, "If the judge bails Charlie to you, you can withdraw your consent at any time. This form tells you the process to have him taken away." We walk her to the door. Zombie-like, we watch as she unlocks her car and drives away.

Although it's a hot day, I shiver. I turn to my husband and ask for what must be the hundredth time. "Are we doing the right thing, do you think?"

He is a kind, generous man. Although he's not my children's biological father, he's welcomed them into his life as he does his own. Even Charlie. He puts his arm across my shoulders. "We can't turn our backs on him. How would we live with ourselves?" We talk again about the potential problems and whether and how we will cope. What boundaries should we insist on? What boundaries will Charlie honour?

I squeeze his hand and sigh. The threatening tears subside. He will keep a level head for both of us. It is comforting leaning on him, totally confident that at last I have a partner who has strengths and a view of the world complementary to my own. At this stage we have been married for eight years and have created a home that we both love. Every item of furniture, every painting, every flower in the garden has been chosen with care and the knowledge that we both love it and that it contributes to this sanctuary of peace and love we have created.

CHAPTER FOUR
Bail is granted

I arrive at the courthouse early. The officers are polite and friendly. I smile, but not with my eyes, as I put my handbag through the security screening machine. The staircase seems longer and steeper today. I tread heavily and at the top I cast my eyes over the waiting area. I sit where my daughter will see me when she arrives.

Charlie's case is called, and we file in. There are not so many people there to support him this time. Charlie wears a different shirt and I wonder where it came from.

A few days ago, Jessica heard he'd collapsed and been taken to the hospital. Fearful his heart problem had resurfaced, I rushed up to see him. I asked for his location at the enquiry counter. The women were helpful and kind and pointed me to the cubicle where I found Charlie being examined.

I slipped around the curtain to see him lying there, hand-cuffed to the bedrail, flanked by two prison guards. "It's my Mum," he raised his head as he saw me. I barely had time to reassure him of my love and intention to bring Jessica to see him. "You can't be here." The guard firmly took my arm and leads me to the other side of the curtain. "He'll be okay," she whispered. My fears settled a little.

I asked her when visiting hours were at the prison. How naive of me. I thought we could just rock up and we'd be allowed to see him. She explained there's a process. "Charlie must put your name on the list for approval. You'll be notified if you are approved." How could I know that? We would have driven the two hours to the prison and been turned away. Now I wonder what else I don't know that I don't know that I don't know.

My daughter prods me. The judge is announced, and we stand. It's a different judge this time and I wonder how continuity is maintained. However, I'm pleased to see a female judge take the bench. Perhaps she will be compassionate.

Charlie's lawyer comes in. Just in time. Again. He takes his place next to the other lawyers in front of the gallery. Protected from us by the screen, can he feel my eyes boring into his back?

The judge addresses Charlie and looks him in the eye as she summarises his alleged crimes and the statutory sentences for each charge. She makes his charges more real to me. She has read the report about bail to our place and tells Charlie he is lucky to have parents who are willing to have him in their home. Most who come before her don't have that support. The recommendation, she says, is to deny bail on the grounds that my husband and I are 'elderly'. My daughters and the others who know us snicker. We are in our 70s. I think of the adverts that declare "70 is the new 50". And I think what a pathetic reason. We are not frail and vulnerable; we are not 'elderly'.

The judge asks if there are other objections to bail being granted. The police have none. She dismisses the comment of our age saying that we are quite capable of withdrawing our consent if it proves too much for us. Charlie is bailed to our place.

It's a party atmosphere as we exit the court and again gather at the roadside. I watch Charlie's lawyer as he comes down the steps.

He nods and moves to pass us by. I stand in his way. "When can I pick up Charlie," I ask him. He says, "Call the prison and arrange a pickup time. Bring him straight home. No visits. No shopping. No stops. Once he's at home he will be visited by the security firm to have his electronic anklet fitted." That's news to me. I thought he'd have it fitted at the prison. "Later a Corrections Officer will visit him to let him know the terms of bail." Simple, but I would never have known. "Charlie is not to associate with drug colleagues. Neither is he to leave the property without permission. Permission will be granted to go to the doctor or visit his lawyer." I step out of his way. Now I'm prepared. I hope.

·····•••·····

"Do you want me to come with you?" my husband asks. I nod.

He drives. As we enter the motorway, my phone rings. It's Jessica. "What time can I pick Charlie up, do you know?" Sweat beads on my forehead. My hands shake as I connect the phone to the car speakers.

"Sorry, Jessica. We're driving. What did you say?" My husband raises his eyebrows and shakes his head as he listens to her repeat the question. My breathing eases as he rests his hand on mine.

"We're on our way to get him. I'll let you know when we're ready for you to visit him." I hope my voice is strong.

"Where did she get that idea from?" I try to be calm. "He's bailed to our place!" I scan the earlier discussion at the courthouse. What led her to this conclusion? Would she be at the prison before us?

"Oh, dear." I take a deep breath. "It would be disastrous. He'll end up back in jail if she gets him."

I ring the prison again and tell them not to release him to her. They confirm he will be released only to us. "After all, he is bailed to your place, not hers," the voice is reassuring.

We take the exit to the prison and soon I phone our arrival to the guardhouse. They get him ready for release. It seems like an hour, but as he reaches us, accompanied by the guard, I glance at the time. It's been fifteen minutes.

Now the fun begins. At least, I'm hoping it will be fun.

Charlie asks if we can stop for KFC. I say no, the instructions are that we are to go straight home. He's like a child. I'm back being the bossy mum. I respond the same to his request for cigarettes. I tell him I'll get some for him later.

"Where's Jessica?" he asks. I say, "I'll call her when you're settled." In my mind that will be in a day or so.

"Jessica wanted to pick you up," I try to ease his disappointment.

"I thought she would get me. I asked her to." He taps at the base of my seat with his foot and drums his fingers on the armrest.

I can't respond to this. All the things I planned to say jumble in my throat. I'm grateful that my husband engages in small talk. Charlie joins in. Soon we arrive at our modest 60s bungalow. Charlie's room was a vibrant blue when we bought the house a couple of years ago. We painted it a warm grey, replaced the venetians with roman blinds and curtains and revamped the wardrobe. This is our guest room. Charlie was not a guest we expected. With a queen-sized bed, side tables and drawers, vibrant prints on the wall, I'm satisfied we've given him a cosy room. We love our home but suddenly it feels too small.

I call the security firm. We sit on the back deck to wait. I'm serving tea when Jessica and her friends arrive. They slap Charlie on the back and shake his hands, obviously glad to see him. I notice his shoulders relax. These are people he knows. We are the strangers here. They love him. Our love is unproven. Or perhaps in his eyes, proven false?

Jessica spreads a picnic of KFC out on the steps. They sit and eat, and she gives Charlie a packet of tobacco, papers and a lighter. Eyes narrowing, he shrugs a shoulder at me.

I am afraid. Something just happened and I don't know what. Oh, how ignorant I am. One day I'll put all this together and then I'll know.

I tell Jessica she can return later. I give her a time. But she and the others must go now. I explain it's a condition of bail.

"That's not the rules!" Charlie towers over me, fingers bunched. I get angry too. I turn to the others. I demand they leave. "Right now!"

As they scuttle away, I turn to Charlie. "I know what I was told is not what you want to hear. We'll sort it out with the

Corrections Officer when she comes. For now, we need to be alone when the security people arrive."

The security people arrive at last. It's hard to watch Charlie fitted with the cumbersome electronic monitoring anklet. A Bluetooth device is placed in a cupboard near the door and its signal tested throughout the property. Outside the house, Charlie is allowed to be in the garage and go to the mailbox but no further. I absorb the instructions. He's shown how to keep the anklet battery charged. He's given a number to call to arrange permission to travel away from the property. I'm given a number to call if there are any problems. I store it on my phone.

It is three days before the Corrections Officer comes. Until then, Charlie remains angry and resentful. To him, I am playing at gatekeeper, using my own ideas to control him. To me, he is like a sullen teenager, not an adult in his 40s.

··········

I look forward to our first meal together and the opportunity to tell him we will support him while he's waiting for sentencing. Charlie helps lay the table. "Jessica can stay a couple of nights a week," I say. I know it must be hard for them to be apart. I look over at my husband and know I'd be devastated if we had no choice about being together.

Right on dinner time, Jessica arrives. I set an extra place. Gone is our alone time with Charlie. She is not offensive, just intrusive. She seems respectful, except she shouldn't be here. She eats everything I offer. She sits close to Charlie. Charlie is relaxed but barely talks.

I'm clearing the table when Jessica looks up into my eyes. "Can I please stay tonight?" I feel Charlie watching for my reaction. I'm tired. I can't say no. We can sort this out tomorrow, I think.

I didn't know it then, but Jessica moved in that night. She had her belongings in her car.

A few days later, the cat came. "Just until I find somewhere for him," she pleaded. But no place was found for the cat.

My emotional energy dissipated in my efforts to educate them. I hadn't understood the term "set boundaries" in this context before. To be honest, I didn't ever think it would be necessary. I developed a repertoire of commands that I used almost hourly.

"The cat is not allowed on the table."

"Feed the cat in the laundry, not in the bedroom."

"Take the cat outside to do its business. Not on paper in the bedroom."

Charlie became the principal cat caregiver while Jessica slept late. She looked and acted like a sleep deprived teenager. Tousled head, she'd come out for breakfast long after the kitchen was cleaned and tidied. She'd eat and go back to bed. At least Charlie cleaned up after her.

Three or four times a week I heard about Jessica's detox 'success'. Detox at our place was easy, apparently. Gratitude for our support poured out of her.

As I write this, it is hard to believe how gullible I was. I'd been warned by everyone I met, but I'd never experienced anything like this, and nothing could prepare me for the reality.

I suppose I'd known peace, once upon a time. But peace eluded me while Charlie was on bail. Broken sleep became the pattern. Jessica never came in by ten, even though that was the 'rule'. Murmuring voices often woke me around 2 am. The morning I found flower petals leading across the front deck to Charlie's window and scattered on his bedroom floor I was livid. I'd long suspected she climbed in through the window at night because she never appeared on the cameras we installed that just missed his window. The flowers confirmed my suspicions, and I could now 'educate' her on the purpose of doors to enter the house, not windows.

False or real, I saw threats everywhere. Strange cars seemed to roam the street at night. Night after night a car backed into the drive across from us. I tried taking photos to get the number plate and make of car but as soon as I pointed the camera through a slit in the curtain, the car moved on. Finally, I asked Charlie about it and the next night he watched and solved the mystery. The paper delivery man did his rounds, not in daylight on the bicycle as in days gone by, but by car in the early hours of the morning.

·····•••···

I want to trust Charlie. The reality of the man driven by addiction isn't yet superimposed on the little boy memories I have of him. We invite Nina and Peter to dinner a few times. Nina always cooks something to contribute to the meal. She is always late, and my portion of the food is always overcooked and inedible. She thinks she is a good cook, but I don't like her food. She spends most of the evening outside on the deck with Charlie. "Talking sense into him," she says. Peter keeps my husband and me company. After a while, I stop inviting them. I need to know what they are talking about, and I refuse to snoop. And I'm getting intolerant of pretending to like her food. Easier not to invite them.

I believe Charlie when he says the people coming to see him are not involved in the drug scene. Some of them interact with us, some ignore us. Gorgeous looking people, well mannered, well dressed, most of them. None raise my suspicions. I didn't know then that none were free of the drug scene, being either users or dealers.

One man, Bill, is very well dressed and talks good naturedly with my husband about his work. His car is out of commission, so Charlie lends him his. We find out later that Bill uses it to deliver and pickup drugs in a run he operates within a six-hour radius of our hometown. Months later, when Charlie is back in prison, the car is finally recovered after Peter concocts and successfully implements an elaborate plan, including the cooperation of a police officer in a nearby town. The police officer convinces Bill it is better to give Peter the car than to be arrested for car conversion.

···········

One day, Jessica's mother and stepfather bring a trailer of motorbikes and lawnmowers for Charlie to work on. There is no room for so many items in the garage and I say so. The stepfather tries to convince me. I ignore him and tell Charlie to choose one thing to work on. The rest are to go.

While Charlie is making his choice, Jessica's mother and I are having a quiet conversation about the healing properties of euphorbia, commonly called milkweed, that grows wild in our garden. She wonders if it would help her wounds on her arms. I explain that we use it to treat skin cancer and it would depend on what her wounds were caused by. Without warning, she turns to Charlie, points at me and calls out, "I'm sick of people saying these dog scratches on my arms are from using P!"

Charlie turns on me, "You have no idea, Mum! It's not even called P!" He looks like the older version of that teenager who told me to "F#*k off out of my life".

I put my hand up to stop him and turn to Jessica's parents. I order them off the property. "And never come back here again!" I don't know what our neighbours are thinking about raised voices from our usually quiet, peaceful place.

Charlie is not happy. Neither am I. He yells. I yell too, "You need to stop and calm down!" When he continues, I say, "I'll have to cancel your bail if you don't stop."

He doesn't stop. I call the number and tell them to come and get him.

He puts his own phone in his pocket as I come back outside. "I've rung Jessica. She'll take me to the police station." He glares at me. "You are just like Granny. And just like her, your kids will leave you and you'll die a lonely old woman too!"

I steel my heart. He won't see how his words cut through me and how they echo my own fears.

Jessica arrives. Charlie opens the car door, starts to get in and stops. Twice. My heart softens. "Do you want a hug?" It seems all I have to offer him now.

"I can give you a hug if you want, Mum." It's a gift he's offering me. If I want it. Not because he wants a hug. We hug and I feel a shift in him.

"You can stay, Charlie. But we need to talk about what just happened."

"Just till I find somewhere else," he says and tells Jessica to go. I call the number again. I assure the woman on the end of the line I'm safe and this is my decision. Charlie stays. He doesn't find another place to serve out his bail time.

The next six weeks are a roller coaster ride, without the exhilaration of knowing it's make-believe and will end in a few moments. But there is no more yelling. Something shifted for me that day. I saw I had it in me to do what feels right for me. It is empowering.

·····•·····

C harlie has a bundle of reports from his lawyer. Police reports about the search and arrest. Copies of his text messages, mainly between him and Jessica, but between others as well. I read them all, with his permission. We are looking for inconsistencies, anything to argue for a reduced sentence.

I'm appalled at what I read. "Why only you, Charlie?" I am still puzzled why the police bypassed others. It's clear from what I'm reading that several other people, including Jessica, have been dealing drugs. I see texts from Nina and see the communications that, to my mind, confirm she was even more involved than being a user.

Charlie was protecting Jessica. That was all he'd admit to. But it was not just Jessica. Charlie was protecting their customers and fellow dealers too. We didn't realise it then. We, and the rest of his family, were also being protected. While he was on bail, Charlie had a visit from a spokesperson from the gang who supplied his drugs. We don't remember seeing anyone who we would identify as being that person. By the time he was sent back to jail, both Charlie and Jessica were adamant that during that visit our protection was negotiated. What was promised or given in exchange, I don't know.

A long time passes before I lose the fear of visitations from the gangs. Or the police.

CHAPTER FIVE

I think I understand

Through the years of our spasmodic connection, I never doubted what a lovely person Charlie is. Kind and generous still, his concern for those who bought the drugs from him was touching. Misguided, but touching.

We are sitting on the deck, he smoking, me having my early morning chai. "You don't know their stories, Mum. If you did, you wouldn't judge."

Is that how he sees me? Judgemental? He is caught up in what's been reported as one of the most dangerous games, dealing and using a drug with horrific consequences for those who use it and their families. How can I remain neutral?

"I do understand pain and grief, Charlie," He looks hard at me and nods.

If only we can have the conversation that is in my heart. My throat is blocked by grief. His ears are too, I think. And I am afraid. Afraid for him and what the future will be like for him. Afraid that if I speak from my heart he won't understand and will throw his own pain at me, pain he believes I caused him.

And no doubt I had caused him pain. Isn't that what every parent has to deal with, almost daily? Memories, either our own, or those of our children, of how we failed in our parenting. It doesn't do any good to remind myself I did my best. I did. I know I did. But it doesn't mean my kids escaped the same sort of trauma and pain that I'd experienced growing up.

Charlie smokes. I've often thought of smoking as a smokescreen. What is Charlie hiding from within himself, behind the screen of smoke he's creating around himself? I eat chocolate. And peppermints. And ginger nuts. No smokescreen for me, just a stuffing down of sweet stuff to keep the bile from boiling up to the surface. Bile. Generated by the liver, its purpose is to aggressively burn fats. That's what I read on Google. I don't think of bile that way when I imagine stuffing myself with sweets to subdue the bile. I don't really mean bile, do I? It's fear and anger accumulated and unresolved from unspeakable experiences in the past. The upshot is, I too am an addict. My addiction is just more socially acceptable. Easier to hide with fewer public consequences. I can go to the grocery store and stock up on boxes of chocolates, packets of biscuits, lollies galore ... fill my trolley to the brim and nobody will think or say anything to indicate they are aware I am feeding an addiction. The checkout operator joins in my jokes about preparing for a kid's birthday party.

How to share all this with Charlie? My own addictions, and the events at the root of them? I can't. My experiences are 'unspeakable'. And some aren't even mine, but ones I've witnessed, as a helpless bystander. I've rarely spoken about my life to Charlie. I've rarely spoken about my own addiction to anyone.

Is it important to share my own addiction with others? Or the events and experiences that drive me there? It's easy to say "Nah.

Who's interested anyway? Why spoil someone's day?" But what good does that do today, for my connection with Charlie? Does he want a connection with me? Sometimes I think so, like today when we are sitting on the deck, trying to talk about why he's involved in not just taking drugs, but in dealing too?

I completely understand why Charlie might use drugs. I also believe Charlie can stop if he wants to. He doesn't want to. Like I don't want to quit sugar. Like me, he has memories and feelings that haunt him. He blames himself for Johnny's death. He fed him and put him to bed that night. I use sugar to stuff down my own memories and emotions, my own feelings of guilt. Charlie uses drugs to deaden his loss and guilt.

Neither of us can face talking about the horror of our demons, not yet. I see this moment is not about me and I let go of my desire to share.

We sit in silence, he smoking, me drinking chai. Like a kaleidoscope, scenes rotate in my mind. I feel guilty for the pain I've caused so many people, not just Charlie. How to share any of that with him? I don't know how to reach him. And I feel guilty about my inability to offer pearls of wisdom that will help him grow and make sense of his choices and, yes, change. I am helpless to help him change.

He sees himself as a supplier who is kinder than most, not charging too much, allowing his clients time to pay, supplying a quality product. He wouldn't take physical actions against people. What he doesn't tell me is the deal he has with his own suppliers who are not so kind-hearted.

Nor does he tell me yet about his gambling. I haven't yet learned that abstinence from one addiction does not necessarily mean addiction-free. Often one substance is substituted for another. Charlie gave up alcohol and cannabis years ago, but Charlie didn't give up addiction. He substituted with methamphetamine, and gambling, and, of course, he never quit tobacco.

There is a long, hard road to travel before I come to this understanding. First, Charlie goes back to court to plead his case.

CHAPTER SIX

Charlie makes a decision

·····•·•····

C harlie's birthday is the day of his court appearance. Before he leaves for court, we give him a pounamu we
bought for him in Rotorua. The design, we were told, sym-
bolises spiritual strength and leadership. Charlie has potential
for both, and we hope he is inspired to enhance these innate
qualities over the months ahead. He seems moved by our gift.

·····•·•····

L ong past the time they are due in the courtroom, the
lawyer, Charlie and Jessica are locked away in a little room
next door. Frustrated at not knowing what is holding them up,
I join them.

His lawyer is encouraging Charlie to plead guilty. There are
benefits, he says. The total sentence time Charlie is facing is
over two years. This means he will serve almost all the time
sentenced. An early guilty plea, that is, pleading guilty today,
will significantly reduce the sentence and therefore the actual
time he serves. Hopefully, though not guaranteed, the sentence

will drop to less than two years. This would mean Charlie would only be in prison for one year.

Charlie doesn't want to go to jail at all. He thinks he should plead not guilty and take his chance with a jury. The lawyer isn't hopeful that this is a good strategy. Since it's so close to Christmas, and the prisons are short staffed over the holiday period, the lawyer expects Charlie will be allowed to continue his bail at our place. He admits that, if he pleads guilty there is a slim chance Charlie will go back to prison to await sentencing. My opinion is not sought. Charlie and Jessica huddle and Charlie decides to plead guilty.

Again, it's a different judge. The hearing commences by the court officer reading the list of offences. It's a long list.

"How do you plead, guilty or not guilty?" He asks after each charge.

Charlie pleads guilty to each charge.

I am suffocating.

As Charlie's lawyer is asking for him to be allowed to remain at our place under the same conditions of bail, the judge interrupts. "This is not going to happen. Trust has been broken." I wonder if the judge is talking about trust in Charlie or the lawyer.

Charlie is remanded to prison until sentencing when he will be brought before the court again. No date is set. I slump forward. My daughter rubs my shoulder. "He'll be all right, Mum." But it's not right to take him away now, on his birthday, before Christmas, when he can be with his family, where I can control the space, no drugs, no mates. Just his family. I take it as a sign. Part of me knows she's right. But that part of me that wants to scream at the judge knows it won't ever be all right. I fear we've lost Charlie.

Charlie said he feels shame around us. And I know he feels misunderstood. I had hoped Christmas would show him we understand more than he thinks. It was an opportunity for us to prove our love is more than rhetoric. The judge's decision took that opportunity away. Away from Charlie. Away from us.

I thought I gave up thinking 'if only' and 'what if' a long time ago. But not today. As I write this, I can't help but think *What if he had come home until sentencing? Would we have been able to reach him, give him an alternative connection to cling to in the months ahead?* I don't know. I do know this: that part of my heart that belongs to my boy is permanently fractured.

·····•··•·····

We stand around, hoping for a last word with Charlie. Jessica gives a bag of his clothes to the guard. We hear Charlie has been taken away to the prison. We leave the court-house.

Sad as I feel, I acknowledge I'll be glad to have our space to ourselves, to regroup and plan what our next steps will be. I tell Jessica I'll pack her things and arrange a time for her to collect them.

CHAPTER SEVEN

The (False) Empowerment of Action

At home, I try to write a list. Lists are empowering. The very act of writing gives me a sense of purpose, of achievement. Things that ordinarily would be done as soon as I thought of them make it to the list. When I put a line through 'Check the mailbox' I get a sense of achievement, of progress, that I am getting something done.

I'm amazed at how much Jessica crammed into Charlie's room. And how little he has. And at how stylish her clothes are and how unkempt and ragged are his. I wonder why Charlie has so little. I pack his things in a small box and put it in the store cupboard.

I neatly pack Jessica's clothes and turn to other items. Books and pens. Cat's dishes and toys. I put these into her laundry basket. I place a Sistema container of tobacco about a quarter of the way from the top. I think it's a strange way to store tobacco but I'm not a smoker, so what do I know? I shrug. Towels and linen fill the basket.

Jessica is late. I have an appointment. I leave my husband to see she gets her things. He rings to ask me where the tobacco container is. Of all her things, that's the only concern Jessica has. I wished I'd kept some of it back. What is in that container with the tobacco? I'll never know, but I suspect.

·············

J ust before Christmas I get a letter from Charlie. From the prison. This and future letters from him will have this message stamped on the back:

This letter is from someone in prison. If you do not wish to receive this mail, please contact the prison at ...

The blood drains from my face. How's our privacy safeguarded here? At every turn I am confounded in my attempts to get information through the system because of the privacy laws. He is allocated an identification number that is to be used to email him, a PRN it's called. I ask for the number but it's a privacy issue. Charlie is the one to give it to me. Charlie must tell me the email address as well. The lawyer is no easier to deal with. Throughout the next year, a series of reports are compiled to support his case for release. Charlie gives me permission to have copies of them. He writes to his lawyer and tells him to give me the reports. But the lawyer refuses to release each document until Charlie again authorises the release of each individual report to me. A one-off blanket approval, which Charlie thought he gave, is not enough. Authorisation is to be by mail because Charlie's lawyer is never available by phone.

But that's in the future. Today, just before Christmas, I receive the first letter from Charlie. I wish I hadn't opened it, a letter so filled with hatred and anger it shocks me still. I felt all the hateful things he wanted to say in person were in that letter. He hates me for kicking Jessica out when I know she has nowhere to go. He looked to me to be a mother figure for her, to love her, and to guide her. I betrayed him. I know she doesn't have a mother who can teach her life skills. I was supposed to be that person for her. That's the essence of the letter, punctuated with examples of my selfishness and failure.

I'm dumbfounded. During the past six weeks, neither of them uttered one word of these expectations about Jessica staying after he went into prison. My husband helps me see the irrationality of Charlie's mind. "There's no rhyme or reason for what he's said. It's the addiction. Don't take it personally."

I turn my energies back to my list. I ignore nagging thoughts of how I failed Jessica. I can deal with physical things. What can I do first? Charlie's house is sitting empty. Charlie realised prison would be his home for the next year or more and agreed to renting it out. But the house is a mess. Not just from the police search but also from a lack of maintenance. There's work to be done.

·········

I walk the short distance from our place to Charlie's house.

While she lived there, Jessica tried to clean but her efforts were scattered, nothing important being achieved. She and her friends broke up concrete paths and levelled the front yard. But they didn't clean the house. Nor, incidentally, did they dispose of the concrete.

People are keen to help but everyone, including my husband, has work or family responsibilities. I am the only one fully retired. I spend hours at the house, cleaning, sorting, throwing things away. I am paranoid about safety and lock myself in the house. Ironically, for the first time ever, I begin to think of myself as elderly. Perhaps that Corrections Officer was clairvoyant.

CHAPTER EIGHT

I am busier

Peter offers to store the remainder of Charlie's possessions. I meet him at the storage place. Noting that the unit is spacious and secure, I return to Charlie's house. While we are loading a trailer at his home, the neighbour tells us she has Charlie's TV, rescued by her sons the day the police arrested Charlie. It's a relief to know the remainder of Charlie's things are now safely stored away.

My daughter and I decide cosmetic changes are enough to prepare the house for rent. Rehang kitchen cupboard doors. Clean the oven. Reglue peeling wallpaper. Replace broken light fittings. Maybe sand and polish the floors. Maybe paint. Certainly, give the house a thorough clean.

The list gets longer, no matter how much I do. Broken concrete from the paths is scattered everywhere. The vegetable garden is overgrown with weeds. The motor and pipes in an outside shed that housed the spa have been stripped. A lean-to at the back of the garage is full of rubbish. Removal of the security cameras attached to the house; clearing the yard and outbuildings go on the list. The spa building is lopsided. Should it go or stay? I don't know. I put it on another list to discuss with my husband. He'll be doing the work.

It's pseudo relief, this list writing business. I'm powerless and I know it. I escape for a while and meet my friend Mary for coffee. We're joined by her friends, a father and son who are property developers. They are interested in Charlie's house. I invite them to have a look. They offer to clear the property of everything back to a bare section for $12,000. I know I can't do all this work, even with the help of others. Their offer gives me an option. Later I realised that was indeed a generous offer.

··········

With regard to methamphetamine use, there's a conflict of views from the former residents. Charlie says they only used in the garage. Jessica says only the bedroom. The flatmate says in the lounge. I'm beginning to think that a cosmetic change will not suffice. It's clear from how I am affected, the house is contaminated. My skin itches. My head aches. But is it from contamination or stress?

My daughter manages rental properties. We discuss the potential for physical methamphetamine related damage. She anticipates a deep clean is all that will be needed. I finally agree and she organises the cleaning materials.

It's not just the effects of methamphetamine use that contaminates Charlie's house, though. The negative emotional energy that's plagued him over the years haunts me every time I go there. One day, locked in, tired and scared, I wander from room to room, taking inventory and adding to the ever-present lists, trying to control my tears. *How will the house ever be ready to rent?*

My phone rings. It's a video call from Darrius, my grandson in Europe. Immediately I feel less alone. He has a gift for calling at the right time, even though this time he's on a first date. I'm grateful he's tuned into my need today. We talk for half an hour. I let it all out, how alone and afraid I am and how much needs to be done and how I don't really know where to start. And he cheers me up. By the time we sign off, my energy levels are higher and I approach the work with a lighter heart.

About fifteen minutes later a knock at the door jars me out of my reverie. I hesitate and ask the caller to identify themselves.

"It's Darrius's cousin, Van. He said you need help."

Tears again, this time of gratitude. Van cheerfully installs the new cistern I'd bought for the toilet and goes through the house attending one by one to several items on my list. Then a quick hug and he is gone.

Darrius's call that day returned me to a degree of equilibrium. The next few months bring some of the hardest choices and decisions I ever make on behalf of one of my children. Darrius showed me I am loved and cared for. His call was evidence of that innate awareness of the cord that binds us together, that makes us family, that prompts us to make that call and, having made the call, gives us the insight to know what to do for the best. Thank you, Darrius.

·····•·•····

I first met Jessica's father a year or so earlier on a rare visit to Charlie. Her father and his two dogs, who ruined his housemate's furniture, had been evicted and he had just moved in with Charlie. "He's got nowhere else to go, Mum," Charlie accepted this man and his situation unconditionally. He moved his own few precious items into his bedroom, kept the door closed, and Jessica's father and his dogs had the run of the rest of the house. No problem for Charlie.

I remember this episode as I arrive at the house to find Jessica's father, homeless again, asleep, camping in Charlie's garage. I look around and am thankful that there are no dogs. I wake him. He shakes himself out of the makeshift bed, "I've got a job," he says. "I want to rent the house. Jessica said it would be all right."

"You can't be here," I say.

I'm sorry for him but this is not where he belongs. He must go.

Another day, I find Jessica and her mates camping out in the house. They are adult women in their twenties acting like messy teenagers, unthoughtful of others. I kick them out. They subject me to verbal abuse as they leave.

Jessica's mother and stepfather arrive in that same week. Her mother lets him do the talking, thank goodness. I know I can't be civil to her. They want to rent the house. The answer is no, of course. Fearing immediate repercussions if I give an outright refusal, I say I'll think about it. I text my decision the next day. Later, when I tell Charlie what I've done, he agrees that it would be difficult for me to be their landlord. Although justified in my refusal, I am still nervous of repercussions. I organise a lock-smith to change the locks.

Cleaning and tidying seem to be taking forever. We gather helpers and finally my daughter declares it enough. I am still sceptical, still itchy and finding it hard to breath in the house. I hope it's due to stress and fear.

My daughter has friends whose children are looking for a place to rent. When they come to inspect the house, the younger son has a reaction like mine and they decide the house is not for them. It's clear to me now that we need to test the extent of contamination.

·········

I call the testing company. The results are staggering. There's no evidence of manufacturing of methamphetamine on the property but the results are as high as if there were. I engage a decontamination company. The company cleans. We get a retest. The house fails and the decontamination company returns. We get three cleanings and three retests and still the house is still contaminated. Finally, we agree to replace the architraves, the cause of the final failed test, and the company signs off.

This process alone costs over $50,000. My husband and I are paying for everything, intending to recoup from the anticipated rent. But there is more work to do before we can rent the house.

The decontamination process strips the wallpaper and disposes of contaminated fittings. Curtains, floor coverings and the kitchen cupboards are among items that go.

COVID-19 arrives and we are in lockdown. Decontamination can be carried out as an essential service. My husband and I can continue our work on the house, but reconstruction work, anything that requires a tradesperson, must wait. It's just my husband and me now. We try to protect ourselves from any residual contamination. We wear gloves and wash our hands often. There is no way we can really know whether we are safe. Certainly, we don't use the same protective gear the professional decontamination team used.

We work companionably as we plan the work. My husband does the bulk of the physical work. I pick up, tidy and dispose of the rubbish. We dismantle the shed, tidy the yard, and clean the garage. Everything goes into big skip bins that will eventually go to the tip with the contaminated material from the house. We restore the gardens, and a new letterbox is installed. From the outside the house is looking cared for.

We look for a builder and find one in the neighbourhood. He agrees to work weekends for us and once restrictions are lifted, he starts work.

With COVID restrictions lifted, prison visits resume. I discuss every major thing I plan to do to the house with Charlie. Sometimes he agrees with me, sometimes I change the plan a little. We are committed to meeting all government regulations for a warm and dry rental house. Our youngest daughter helps design the kitchen.

It's a demoralising time for Charlie. I understand he feels powerless and try to give him autonomy in those areas I am managing for him. Even so, it's a struggle to keep his interest in the house alive. It holds many good memories for him, but the saddest things hold the greatest power. He is angry I went ahead with the decontamination. It's hard to comprehend that he wasn't aware of the extent of methamphetamine use in his own home.

The cost of decontamination is high. The cost of restoration will be higher. And it's unlikely Charlie will return to the scene of his offending. His children have no sentimental attachment to the house. He agrees to sell and grants power of attorney to his daughter and me.

I think it will be an easy process to arrange the power of attorney. I get my lawyer to draw up the documentation. But my lawyer won't visit the prison. Charlie's lawyer is his court appointed, government paid, legal aid lawyer. Not once has he visited Charlie, so I don't even think to seek his help. I ask another lawyer who has the same response as my lawyer. But her daughter is a criminal lawyer. She gets her to ring me.

Jane is compassionate and efficient. She does the job for the same fee she would get for her legal aid work. Within 24 hours, she picks up the documents and meets with Charlie. The original documents, signed, together with several copies are delivered to me the same day. It feels like a major milestone, and it proves to be. That power of attorney document opens doors that were closed before. Now we can act on Charlie's behalf as far as his property is concerned.

Charlie is excited when I see him next. When they met, he realised he knows Jane. She exudes competence and that generates confidence. How we wish he could have had her as his court appointed lawyer.

········

When we tell the builder we are going to sell, he introduces us to his friend, Mick, who is looking to buy in the area. While Mick raises the finance, we continue with our plans.

Mick's father paints. The builder adjusts our plans to accommodate a few structural changes Mick wants. We are taking a risk, allowing more extensive renovations, but we like this young man. He will more easily get finance for a habitable house than the way it is now. He's taking a risk too, and so's his father. If Mick doesn't get finance, the expenses and labour they've invested will not be recovered.

We order the kitchen, air conditioner, underfloor insulation, bathroom light and extractor fan. Mick is happy with our choices and our builder proceeds with installation. The electrician and plumber are engaged and soon the house is ready for the bank inspection. Mick and his parents come to see us. We have a price we hope to achieve for the house. Mick is limited by how much he can borrow. He tells us his top offer. It's close enough to our price that we agree the sale. Mick is overjoyed. We are too.

Freedom of the worries about Charlie's house brings relief that our expenses are recovered. My energy begins to return and, with more time available, I can now concentrate on getting him support.

CHAPTER NINE

Prison life

I struggle to find the best way to support Charlie as he waits for his sentencing hearing.

Communication is difficult. I'm finally given his prison email address. He doesn't have access to the internet and the emails are printed off and given to him. I wait to receive his letters in reply. There's a process to follow for everything. Charlie doesn't know these processes. I research and email him instructions. There are forms to be filled out and signed by him. I am told all this information is displayed in several places throughout the prison. Charlie doesn't see them. I tell him who in prison to ask for the forms. I email him phone numbers and addresses he asks for, including my own so he can get permission to call people. I get used to the waiting. I am busy but Charlie is always in my thoughts.

Once he can make calls, I hear from him. Mostly it's when he wants some items to make his life more comfortable. I wait for the prison letter giving me permission to visit. I hope Charlie won't refuse me as a visitor. The letter arrives and I settle into a pattern of weekly visits. I follow the prison process every week to get permission to visit. I call between certain hours, leave a message, state Charlie's name and PRN and the day and time of the visit and wait for a confirmation call. I'm starting to recognise the voices of the officers who call to confirm my visiting times. I try to match the voices with the faces that greet me when I arrive. I play games with myself. How many smiles will I give before I get a smile in return.

But there's something I never succeed in turning into a game. Will Charlie be pleased to see me? He is never pleased to see me. Prisoners are told they are to get a visit, not who the visitor is. Even though I write and tell him when to expect me, my heart catches at the disappointment on his face when he realises it's me and I'm alone. Jessica rarely comes - with me or on her own. My heart shrivels a bit more each time.

"It is what it is, Mum," he says when I try to engage him in a discussion about why Jessica doesn't visit.

After a few minutes catching up, we settle down to what is usually a pleasant chat. I hear about his cellmate and how embarrassed Charlie is about his own snoring. I empathise with his cellmate. Even though we closed our bedroom doors, his snoring could wake me.

Charlie has found a knowledgeable support network amid his fellow prisoners. The advice from this quarter is freely given and includes who is the best lawyer. He hears he should never have agreed to plead guilty. He's not happy with his lawyer, and to be honest, neither am I. He's heard about a lawyer in Auckland who might be able to rescue the situation. "I'll contact him and see what can be done," I tell him. I ask the guard for a pen and write the lawyer's name on my hand.

·········

I make an appointment and take the trip to see what we hope is to be Charlie's new lawyer. The bus gets me there a little early so I sit in a café before making my way to the lawyer's rooms, arriving punctually. I want to make a good impression.

I've researched this lawyer, so I recognise him as I reach his door. He shows a young man out and I introduce myself. "You shouldn't come early to your appointment." He is clearly agitated.

I try to look at my phone to check the time, but he stops me. "Go get a coffee and come back when it's time. That man has just come off the plane from China and should be wearing a mask." He shuts the door and I'm left in the hall.

I'm so tempted to catch the next bus home. So far, we have escaped this new pandemic and the whole country is nervous. If COVID-19 has visited his office, do I want to be here? But I'm paralysed by his rudeness. I am not early. And I certainly don't need a coffee. I pace the hall until I think enough time has passed for him to be less agitated.

Finally, I return to his office. I am invited in and seated opposite him in what appears to be his waiting area. He is certainly more friendly, less flustered now. He may have apologised for his rudeness, but I don't remember. He seems to think he'd be able to make a difference for Charlie. I hope he will organise to take over as Charlie's court appointed lawyer. He does undertake court appointed work, I know that from his website. But no. He says he needs a separate engagement and will be sending an estimate of costs along with the letter of engagement – to Charlie – not to me, even though it will be me and my husband who will be paying his bill. He's friendly enough, but I'm disappointed. I leave his office frustrated. Again proving to be powerless to help Charlie.

When the letter comes to Charlie, he is furious. The new lawyer wants a $17,000 retainer fee on the understanding the final bill could be more. What price freedom? Not one Charlie wants to commit to. On Charlie's instruction, I tell the lawyer "Thanks, but no thanks". That's the outcome I anticipated from Charlie when the Auckland lawyer wanted a private engagement. Interesting fact: this lawyer's name is often in the media cited as representing many of those arrested on drug offences. I remain curious as to what the outcome for Charlie might have been had he signed the offer of engagement.

·····•·····

Prisoners are resourceful. "I've learned at least seventeen new skills," Charlie tells me. I ask him which of these he thinks might lead to a new career. "None! None of them are legal!" He enjoys his joke. I enjoy seeing the sparkle of the young Charlie. And I despair. The courses and prison work opportunities supposedly available for prisoners are available only when they are sentenced, not when on remand. Charlie is on remand for six months. All this time in high security. Six months with no opportunity for growth and healing and preparing for a change of life. Six months with limited time outdoors. Six months to learn these new 'skills' he talks of, to make new connections. With no sentence date set, I fear that his fate may be to be kept on remand indefinitely, as sometimes happens.

·····•·····

"It is what it is," is something he says often. In considering the sale of his house: "It is what it is." A sentence could be imposed that is up to the fullest extent under the law the judge can impose. "It is what it is." Jessica's visits are few and far between. She may not be there for him when he is released. "It is what it is."

While I admire anyone who can accept life's challenges, I am frustrated by this fatalistic acceptance. He knows it's his actions and decisions that have put him in prison, but he doesn't see fault in those decisions and actions. I think he honestly believes he had valid reasons and this both puzzles and scares me. I come to see I have no influence and no matter what I say or do to help, he won't change. I continue to do my best to help his situation. I pray for him to want to change.

·····•·••···

The COVID-19 pandemic finally arrives in New Zealand in March and soon afterwards, a visitor from overseas shares it with his family member in prison, bringing life inside the prison to a standstill. Prison visits are cancelled for a time. Charlie never catches COVID, a relief to him and us as his heart problem makes him vulnerable.

Because of the pandemic, Charlie's hearing for sentencing is delayed further. He continues to write. I can send some things to him. But there's a process for that. After lots of confusion we develop a system. He rings, tells me what he wants. I send him an email and tell him how to put in a property request and get the prison staff to email their approval to me. I buy what he needs and courier it to him at the prison. I email and tell him it's arriving. Still, there's another step we don't get to know about for months. The items go into his property box and he has to request the items be released to him. This step is not always honoured by prison staff as sometimes he receives items without having to request them.

There are rules around what he can and can't have. No clothing with red or black, no gang insignia, no branded items, including shoes and shirts. He's allowed ten books and five CDs. CDs must be in the original covers, no copies.

He wants an electric razor and a CD player. The approved electric razor type is a corded one. The CD player can't record and can't be remotely operated. Electronic items like these need to be checked and there's a fee for that. Charlie is to request the check and authorise the fee to be taken out of his prison bank account.

Before I know the 'rules' we drive to the prison with a box of things for Charlie. An electric jug is included. We happen to be served by a woman who knows my husband and she kindly explained we must courier everything, not bring it to the prison in person. However, she took it all, receipted it and logged the items. I gave her the money for the examination of the jug. But this leads to more confusion, cleared only when I ring the property officer to see why his items haven't been delivered to him.

Confusion is never fully cleared. He finally receives the razor when he is discharged on parole, months after I'd sent it and too late to be returned for a cordless one as the return by date had expired.

CHAPTER TEN
The Visitor's dilemma

V isiting the prison results in one long battle against the practices and culture within the prison system. Either intentionally or not, these practices make it hard for people to support their family member in prison.

For me, it's a two-hour drive to the prison which is in the middle of farming land over an hour's drive south of Auckland. The prison serves the wider region, and many prisoners have family members living outside the region. The majority of prison visitors travel a long distance for their short visit with their loved ones.

Our visit begins with the simple procedure at reception. Visitors are given a bracelet, like a hospital bracelet, not white but fluorescent coloured, that shows our name and the time of our authorised visit. I've lost count of the number of times I couldn't break it off and had to wait till I got home to use scissors. Several times I still had it on as I went to the supermarket on the way home. On these occasions, I often received knowing looks.

The prison being a men's prison, most visitors are wives and sweethearts and mothers. Everyone puts on a brave face. In a way, I look forward to the discussions with fellow visitors as much as my visits with Charlie. I'm learning I have a lot in common with them.

One woman told me how ashamed she is. "I've told no-one my son's here. None of my friends, no one at work. I work late some days to make up the time it takes to come and visit. When I leave work to come here, they think I'm at the dentist or the doctor."

Another woman tells me, "My brother had been sentenced and I was an approved visitor. I came to visit him from my home 250 kms away (outside the region) on my way to visit family in Auckland. In all, about a five hour drive. I'd been sent information and was there on his visit day. When I got here, I was told I was supposed to call first to make an appointment, but nowhere in my information letter did it say that. 'It must have been left out', she told me. Then she told me to go away and make an appointment and come back another day. I refused, and not politely I assure you, and I said I was staying till I saw him. I'd been awake since 4 am to get there in time for visiting hours. Of course, in the end they let me visit him. But I felt I was worth less than the dirt under that woman's feet at the extra work and inconvenience I'd caused."

Another woman wanted to borrow a phone book and was refused. She exploded. "If it wasn't for us, you wouldn't have a job, so be more civil and stop treating us as if we're scum!" She clenched her fists as she told me this experience.

In most cases I found the staff friendly and helpful. They have their job to do. But, overall, dealing with them felt like negotiating one big obstacle course. Never the athlete, failure seemed inevitable for me. And I'm not the only one. I often bumped into others in the toilets, suppressing their tears and anger, frustrated at the way they were dealt with. None of us wanted to show our vulnerability to the staff.

At a signal from the receptionist, we head off to the guard-house some 200 metres away. It's a nice walk, past a pond where ducks swim. The walls of the prison aren't too imposing. The guards greet us with a spiel about COVID-19 – are we sick, do we have any symptoms, have we been in contact with anyone with COVID etc. Satisfied, he allows us in. We give our names and pass through the security metal detector. At the same time our temperature is taken to be sure we are not sick. I wonder about myself. I have Hashimoto's and as a result, my tempera-ture is normally one or two degrees lower than normal. If I had a temperature, would it show on their device? Satisfied again that we meet the system requirements for entry we either are told to go straight to the visitors' centre or to turn left to be examined by the sniffer dogs. In all the time I come to the prison I have only been subjected to the dog's examination three times. Never is my car searched, although that can happen.

We sit for a while in the waiting room beside the visitors' 'lounge' and then are checked off against the list, told where to sit while we await our family member. Seating is fixed to the floor, three moulded concrete seats in blue for visitors, one in grey for the prisoner. All eyes are on the door to the hall. I get used to the orange jumpsuits zippered at the back. It's not a flattering colour or style. Sometimes Charlie's jumpsuit is too small. He doesn't complain.

I am amazed that the little children don't seem aware. They run to meet their fathers, hugging and kissing and snuggling into their shoulders. It touches my heart. When Charlie's grandson is born his daughter brings him a few times. Then she is back at work and her opportunity to visit is gone. It's a pity because it looked as if Charlie would bond with this little fellow.

Few visitors deliberately flout the rules and when confusion arises, staff do not empathise. Here the guards are extra vigilant. They roam around alert for any abnormalities. If the rules are broken here, swift action is taken. One young couple sitting near me come in for what seems like extra scrutiny and this makes me uncomfortable. When it's time to go, the young woman is asked to stay. Later Charlie tells me she is banned for six months. She wore a lot of jewellery into the prison and when she got up to go, it was clear she had none. She was adept at slipping it off and somehow passing it to her partner. He intended to use it to barter for items in the prison. Apparently, she had done this before.

It's an emotional strain dealing with the visit staff. It takes its toll on me and others. However, dealing with "support staff" inside the prison demands even more of me.

CHAPTER ELEVEN

Remand – internal processes and support

E arly on in his incarceration, Charlie is assigned a case manager. Within the first few weeks, she helps him fill out a form to apply for a three-month residential rehabilitation programme. He is excited and cheered by his meeting with her. She assures him his application will be successful and undertakes to send it away "immediately". The process she outlines includes the judge mandating him to attend this programme as part of his sentence.

But, the residential rehabilitation matter is not even discussed at sentencing. His hope then is that at his parole hearing he will be released early to the programme. Well into his second year in prison and concerned that he hasn't heard from the programme facilitators, he asks me to follow up for him.

The administration person at the facility is encouraging. The facility has a reputation for successful rehabilitation. I like the focus on Māori cultural traditions and way of life as Charlie has always had a respect for Tikanga Māori. Perhaps it's because of his own indigenous roots. Although he is unaware of our

Aboriginal heritage, I recently had occasion to show his photograph to the daughter of an elder from our Wonnarua Mob. She recognised similarities with a particular Wonnarua man. Charlie would have loved to know this. I'm sure it would give him a sense of belonging, as knowing my roots has done for me.

Charlie's not being Māori doesn't seem to be a disadvantage. Although self-referrals are accepted, since Charlie is hoping to attend the programme directly from prison, confirmation won't be given until his parole date is confirmed.

I am asked to send in his application form so they will have it on file. I am surprised and angry that they don't already have his application as Charlie's case manager said she'd forward it early on in his confinement.

I now need to get the application from her and forward it myself. I spend months trying to communicate with her, as does Charlie. When I finally get a copy of the application from her and submit it, I find she has excluded some pages, including those with Charlie's signature. Nothing runs smoothly on this roller coaster ride. The facility is helpful, and, after more toing and froing, we are now hopeful that his application has been received and accepted.

··········

The Criminal Justice Act provides the opportunity for Charlie to request the court to consider a cultural report that outlines his cultural background, personal circumstances, and family situation. I am positive such a report would be helpful as Charlie's involvement with drugs, occurring from a young age, and stemming from the time he went to live with his father, was compounded by the grief over the death of his baby. We have no say over the identity of the report writer and when I learn she is a friend of Charlie's former wife, I engage another person privately and pass this report on to his lawyer.

Three reports are prepared over the time Charlie is in prison. Never does the judge acknowledge the content of these reports or indicate that they are considered in the recommendations and sentencing.

Supposedly to support the recommendations in these reports, his lawyer encourages me to write an affidavit. This is a waste of time, and I wonder why he didn't anticipate the outcome. My affidavit is rejected by the judge as a 'self-referral'. A common occurrence for a family member's affidavit. Who besides his mother would know him and some of the extenuating circumstances? Although I acknowledge I am probably biased, I am devastated at the lack of respect for my integrity. And by this additional evidence of the incompetence of his lawyer.

·········

At first, Charlie is keen to get to training courses. He loses interest when he hears there is a 9-12 month waiting list to be included in the drug treatment unit (DTU), a mandatory course to be undertaken prior to parole being granted. His inclusion in the DTU could be brought forward with intervention from his case manager. She never initiates that intervention.

While he is on remand he is accommodated in the high-risk unit where he meets men with a variety of offending experience. I am pained by the stories he shares with me. These are men, almost all of them, who have experienced loss, grief and abuse in their early lives. Many are mentally scarred. Charlie's concern for them is obvious. I am empathic but must admit I have no energy to take up anyone else's fight. I feel Charlie's disappointment. He knows at a different time I would have done what I could to help.

I encourage him to take up writing again, an activity he used to enjoy a long time ago. I know he has kept a diary, so I buy him another. Perhaps he will put some of these stories and his perceptions to paper.

·········

Charlie is not used to being idle. Being kept in his cell for most of the day is driving him crazy. I can't understand the logic behind keeping grown men unemployed. *The Devil finds work for idle hands* ... What seems hardest for him is every decision is made for him. "You can get used to this life," he tells me. Mealtimes, exercise times, rest times – all are determined by 'the system'. He has no choices to consider; no decisions to make. The only option he has is to be patient – or not.

Once sentenced, Charlie applies for work in the prison and is elated when he is finally given meaningful work, first in the prison kitchen, then as a driver within the prison grounds. He enjoys the comradery of work colleagues. He laughs as he tells me of the antics some of the kitchen hands get up to. I also hear stories of how the gangs are active within the prison. Food is their commodity. I fear for him but he laughs at my fears. "I keep my head down, Mum. Don't worry," he says.

But I do worry. I worry about his safety. I worry that his case manager is not held to account. I worry that her work ethic is harmful to Charlie's future. I worry that he will always be addicted. I worry he will never change.

CHAPTER TWELVE

Parole hearings and Clarity around Charlie's addictions

Once Charlie is sentenced, his original lawyer tells me that his job is done. But there's the matter of parole. Won't he do that? No, he doesn't handle that side of the process. But he recommends 'one of the best' in this field. I copy his name and make contact by email, explaining Charlie's case.

Looking back, I don't know why I contacted Dave on the recommendation of a lawyer I had less than no confidence in. But it proved one of the best decisions. He replied to my email telling me he lived close to us and, since he was a neighbour, did I want to reconsider engaging him? I was overjoyed to have him on board and so began the most rewarding of associations. Not once did we regret Dave's involvement.

Charlie's first parole hearing date looms but parole won't be granted until his prison drug rehabilitation course, the DTU, is completed. Yet Charlie still hasn't been enrolled in the DTU.

At this first parole hearing, each Board member leans forward listening intently as Charlie's daughter, heavily pregnant, lists his qualities as a parent. Despite being impressed by Charlie's daughter, the Board refuses parole. As far as we understand, it's because he has not done the DTU course.

His case manager did not attend the first parole hearing. The Parole Board stated that they were looking to make it mandatory for case managers to be at the hearings. She was the only person in the prison given the responsibility for speaking for him so it was baffling to see how the Parole Board could ascertain Charlie's character without hearing from her.

Charlie finally starts the DTU course. But by the time of his second Parole Board hearing, he still has some weeks to completion. I am gratified to see his case manager is at his second hearing. I can't say if it makes a difference to the decision, but she talks favourably about Charlie's potential for re-offending.

Since Charlie's arrest, it is clear to me that his drug use is linked to past emotional trauma. That this was one of the principal arguments his parole lawyer made to the Parole Board was encouraging and heartening. He argued before the Board that prison was not the place for Charlie and men like him who had suffered trauma. They belonged in the community and with families who could support them in their healing. He also argued a strong case for psychological help, both whilst still in prison and following release. Maybe it was because the parole hearing was held in a small room that I sensed the Board agreeing with his summary. So, when parole was finally granted and the Board didn't state any residential or other rehabilitation courses, or counselling as conditions of parole I was devastated. What chance for change does he have now?

Parole is set to start two months in the future to enable him to complete the course. The only conditions of parole are regular meetings with his probation officer and that he live with my husband and me for the duration of his parole.

Charlie is excited to be paroled. His first thoughts are for me to buy him cigarettes. And he asks me to pick him up some KFC to eat on his release.

I confide in Dave who is also disappointed that Charlie's thoughts are only of satisfying his own appetites. Dave suggests we get KFC and have the release meal together with Charlie, as a family. "That will ground him," he says, "and get him started in the right manner."

Although I am hopeful that Charlie won't relapse, I suspect that, unless he starts thinking of his family, especially his children and his grandson, he won't be successful.

Charlie sees his third Christmas in prison.

CHAPTER THIRTEEN

Rehabilitation after prison

The six weeks having Charlie on bail at our place were harrowing. I could not understand his addiction to methamphetamine. I heard about a charitable organisation called PARS, Prisoners' Aid and Rehabilitation Services, who perhaps could help me make sense of what happened. I sought them out. I learn how to get information about the prison and briefly how to communicate with Charlie once he is incarcerated.

But what I need from them is an understanding of his addiction and the effects of the drugs he's been taking, "I don't know anything about methamphetamine, dear," I am told. Although there is kindness, I am disappointed in her lack of understanding of the drugs that are the cause of so many people being in jail. If Charlie could give up two addictions, why can't he quit methamphetamine? Disillusioned, I don't visit PARS again. I need to find a more informed source. I find more information through Google searches, but these are a poor substitute for human connection.

Some helpful clarification comes from Dave, our parole lawyer. He has a process to support an addict moving through the phases of quitting their addiction. The first, as with all addictions, would be the willingness to quit. All addictions. Charlie doesn't show that willingness. I don't disclose knowledge of Charlie's gambling addiction. I wanted him to discuss it with the report writers, but he refused and asked me to keep it to myself. But now, with this clarification from Dave, I see that Charlie has three major addictions. Not only is he addicted to methamphetamine, but tobacco and gambling also have a major hold. Perhaps these last two are more important to him even than methamphetamine.

During the few months before Charlie's second parole hearing, I begin looking for help for him through the various organisations in the community that offer rehabilitation services. At the same time, I remain hopeful to hear from the first rehabilitation centre.

I look for a place that will accept him as a self-referral. First, I want to know what services they offer him so he can see if it would be a course of action he could follow. I call every agency in our local area and some in Auckland. I always speak to receptionists, never someone who deals with people with addiction. Never anyone who will talk with me face to face. The outcome in every case is the offer to consider him as a self-referral. The catch is he must apply himself. I accumulate a list of addresses for him. He writes to a few and receives less than a handful of replies. None will offer him a place until he has been released on parole.

Knowing his language and writing skills have dwindled through his drug use, I am frustrated in the knowledge I am not allowed to help him seek help. It's impossible for me to help him fill out forms or write letters. Pen and paper are not allowed in our visiting times.

I'm frustrated at the futility of all these calls. Is this generic response from them all because I don't know the questions to ask? If so, I don't get help in framing them from anyone. What do they think of me? What do I sound like to them? Do they hear the broken, dispirited woman I've become, feeling more helpless and more hopeless with every call? I am getting nowhere in my search to help my son. It's been a long time since I felt so invisible, so worthless in my frantic search for help. Feelings of suicide rise to the surface. Somehow, I find the will to try one more time.

CHAPTER FOURTEEN
Help is found

In my search for help for Charlie on his release, the last place I call is CareNZ. It's the last place because, finally, I am invited to sit down with a counsellor and discuss how they can help.

That meeting with Mabruka was a turning point. Not for Charlie, as I expected, but for me. The weight of sorrow and fear I'd been carrying for months began to lift under her gentle words. The dam keeping my emotions in check burst. Mabruka's gentle way of listening and understanding what I said was affirming. She didn't minimise my grief and anguish. She didn't give me false hope. She heard me and when I finally took a deep breath, she invited me to join the Whānau Group –set up to support people supporting a loved one steeped in addiction. Years later as I write these words, tears of gratitude still rise to the surface when I remember how close I came to the end of my endurance.

·····•••·····

Surround yourself with people who get you, back you, believe in you, and make your heart happy Lisa Pollock

My favourite photo of myself is one where I am in my early 50s, taken with my brother and sister on Magnetic Island in North Queensland. I'm happy in that photo. I am content in knowing I am where I belong, with people who I love unconditionally and who love me the same way. I am known and happy to be known, faults and all. I am at peace. Every time I look at that photo those feelings are regenerated.

Being with the Whānau Group revives those feelings. Every Wednesday, in their company, I feel my old self returning, piece by piece. I begin to laugh again - a real belly laugh. And the tears flow freely too. This is my Whānau, my family, every bit as much as my brother and sister are.

Members of the Whānau Group are mothers, grandmothers, siblings, and fathers. All seeking to support a loved one in the throes of addiction. Their stories touch my heart. My story is embedded in one way or another in their stories and mine in theirs. These people are people who know me, who love me, who've got my back, who are rooting for me. I trust them with my fears, my hopes, my grief.

Our beautiful facilitator, Sherryn, both encourages and admonishes us. We learn the meanings of foreign words and phrases like "staying connected", "being compassionate", "I am not the cause", "setting boundaries", and, most foreign of all, "self-care".

Little by little my heart stills and I find peace. Peace in knowing Charlie's addiction is not my fault. Peace in knowing that although I made mistakes in my life, that I did the best I could as a person, as his mother, and that my best is good enough.

I learn to let Charlie (and his choices) go. It's not my place, nor is it my responsibility to bring about change for him. I come to understand what these foreign terms mean for me. I now know that in my trying to care for Charlie first, I'd lost sight of how important it is to care for myself. I learn that self-care is not selfish but is an act of love. In finding joy in every little thing in my day, doing at least one thing that is healing for me, brings me peace and clarity around when and how to help, not just Charlie, but others too. I learn to accept that my help is not always wanted. And that's all right.

Charlie's parole to our place didn't work out for him. In less than a month he left us. He really wasn't there, to be honest. From the second night he went out in his car until early hours of the morning. He helped in the garden cutting down a tree and filling the garden beds with soil we had trucked in. But even though he'd promised to undertake more, no other involvement in our family life occupied his time.

I haven't seen him and only heard from him once in just over two years. I hear about him from time to time. I know he lives in Auckland. Although I doubt he has escaped from his addictions, I do know it's none of my business. My business is to take care of myself and those who welcome me into their lives. My business is to find joy in my life in the face of Charlie's decisions for his own life.

I know Charlie's heart is in the right place. I may judge his activities as being not ones I choose to share. But I do know that whatever he does, his motives are pure. He has a deep capacity for love and, though society may judge him misguided, he only wants what is best for others. And society may judge me misguided too, in my view that, by appearing to turn his back on his own Whānau, Charlie continues to protect us in his way.

My heart embraces him with love. He left our home of his own choice. If/when he chooses to ring our doorbell, he will find the door flung open wide. We will greet him with joy and our arms will embrace him with love.

CareNZ

THE CARENZ CREED

We are here because there is no refuge finally from our-
selves
Until we confront ourselves through the eyes and hearts
of others, we are running
Until we suffer them to share our secrets, we have no safety
from them
Afraid to be known, we cannot know ourselves nor any
other, we will be alone
Where else but on our common ground can we find such
a mirror
Here together we can at last appear clearly to ourselves
Not as the giant of our dreams
Nor the dwarf of our fears
But as a person, part of a whole sharing in its purpose
On this ground we can each take root and grow
Not alone any more as in death, but alive to ourselves and
others.

About Stephanie

S tephanie has written about her experience with compassion and understanding, not just for her son, but for herself and others. While managing her son's material resources she also focused on navigating prison and rehabilitation systems to find support for herself as well as her son.

Her earlier life challenges, such as facing widowhood and divorce, developed resilience and determination. A professional background as a Town Planner gave her techniques to navigate systems. This memoir highlights how one needs courage to find others who have gone before, who can add a layer of support and connection in a way that helps us cope with the shocks life sometimes throws at us. With such support and connection, the path to survival is made clear.

Her story of how she survived, and thrived, gives hope to others caught in the web of addiction, whether they be attempting to support a loved one, or whether they be the substance user.

See more on her website:

www.StephanieHammondAuthor.com

Other Books
by Stephanie Hammond

Novels

Last Days in Atlantis published 2010 (to be republished in 2024)

Children's books

Beatrice the Angel with One Large Wing Series

  1. Beatrice Learns Compassion

  2. Beatrice Learns Joy (to be released in 2024)

To purchase copies, visit the author's website:
www.StephanieHammondAuthor.com

Thank You

I hope this memoir gives you insight and
hope for your own situation.
It would be helpful if you could please visit
www.amazon.com
and write a CUSTOMER REVIEW of the book.
Constructive comments are always welcome.

Sign up for my newsletter to keep in touch
with things I'm doing at
www.stephaniehammondauthor.com
and
Join our FaceBook readers' group at
Stephanie Hammond Readers Group

Made in the USA
Middletown, DE
22 November 2023

43295229R00049